Sacajawea
Translator and Guide

Written by Irene Nakai Hamilton
Illustrated by Troy Anderson

MODERN CURRICULUM PRESS

Program Reviewers

Cathy White Eagle, Executive Director
and President of the Board
Eagle Vision Educational Network
Granite Bay, California

Jeffrey Hamley, Director
Native American Program
Harvard University
Cambridge, Massachusetts

Gwen Sebastian Hill, Teacher
Development Trainer
District of Philadelphia
Philadelphia, Pennsylvania

Paulette Molin, Ph. D., Assistant Dean
The Graduate College
Hampton University
Hampton, Virginia

Joan Webkamigad, Education Specialist
Michigan Department of Education
Lansing, Michigan

Executive Editor: Janet Rosenthal
Project Editors: Elizabeth Wojnar
Mark Shelley

MODERN CURRICULUM PRESS

An imprint of Paramount Supplemental Education
250 James Street
Morristown, New Jersey 07960

ISBN 0-8136-5759-8   (Reinforced Binding)   0-8136-5765-2   (Paperback)
Library of Congress Catalog Card Number: 94-677298

10 9 8 7 6 5 4 3 2 1   SP   99 98 97 96 95 94

Dear Reader,

Have you ever traveled far from home? What kinds of things did you see? Sacajawea helped the explorers Lewis and Clark on their journey across the United States. She had many adventures as their translator and guide.

Read to learn about Sacajawea's life before she met the explorers, and how she helped make their journey a success. As you read, think about some adventures that you have had.

Your friend,

Irene Hamilton

The people of the Shoshoni Nation had their own name for the Rocky Mountains. They called them the "Shining Mountains." Around 1788, a girl named Sacajawea was born in the beautiful "Shining Mountains," near the Lemhi River Valley. This valley is in what is now the state of Idaho.

When Sacajawea, which means Bird Woman, was a little girl, times were changing for the Shoshoni Nation. Settlers were moving to the west and pushing Native Americans off their land. It was a time of fear and sadness for Native Americans.

3

Sacajawea's family, along with the
other members of the Shoshoni
Nation, camped along the banks of
rivers. Living near a river made it
easier to fish for salmon. The men
of the nation also hunted for buffalo
on the plains. Sacajawea helped
her mother when her father and
brother went to hunt buffalo.

6

Sacajawea's mother and grandmother taught her about plants, roots, and berries. They also taught Sacajawea how to clean a buffalo and cook the meat. They showed her how to make clothing and blankets from the buffalo skin. Sacajawea watched and listened carefully.

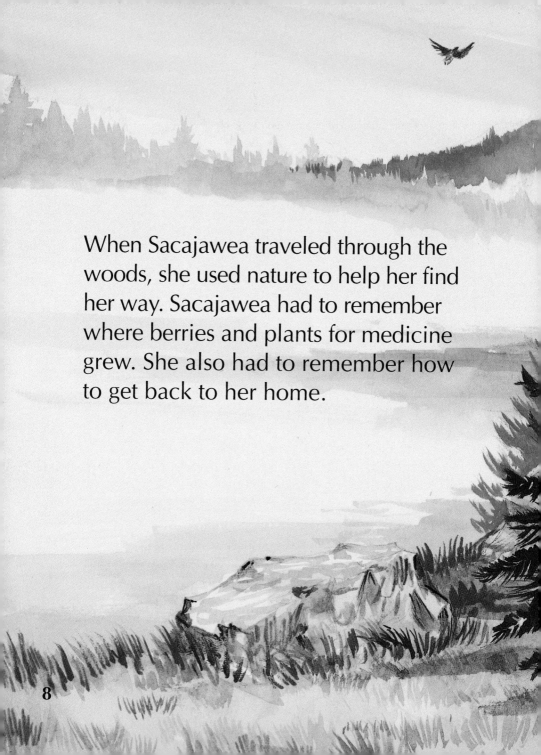

When Sacajawea traveled through the woods, she used nature to help her find her way. Sacajawea had to remember where berries and plants for medicine grew. She also had to remember how to get back to her home.

When Sacajawea was about eleven, her family was camped on the banks of the Missouri River. Another Native American nation, the Hidatsa, attacked them. The Hidatsa kidnapped Sacajawea. She tried to escape but she was caught.

The Hidatsa sold Sacajawea to a French trapper. His name was Toussaint Charbonneau. At first, Sacajawea was very unhappy. She missed her family. But she began to get used to her new life. Toussaint and Sacajawea were soon married.

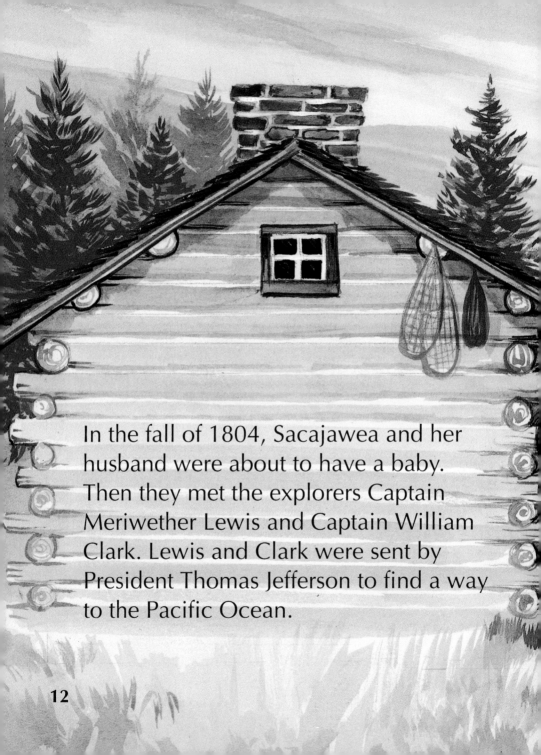

In the fall of 1804, Sacajawea and her husband were about to have a baby. Then they met the explorers Captain Meriwether Lewis and Captain William Clark. Lewis and Clark were sent by President Thomas Jefferson to find a way to the Pacific Ocean.

Lewis and Clark asked Toussaint if he and Sacajawea would go with them on this important trip. They wanted Toussaint and Sacajawea to help them speak with the Native Americans whom they might meet along the way.

In April, 1805, Sacajawea, Toussaint, Lewis, and Clark left Fort Mandan in what is now North Dakota.

Sacajawea and Toussaint brought along their newborn son. His name was Jean Baptiste Charbonneau, but everyone called him Pomp. Pomp would travel the entire 4,000 mile trip with his mother and father.

15

The trip was not easy. The group was often hungry and sick. Sacajawea showed Lewis and Clark which plants were safe to eat. She helped guide them when she could. Her quick thinking rescued important supplies when a canoe overturned in the river.

Sacajawea also saved Lewis and Clark from being attacked. Other Native American nations knew that the group did not mean harm. This was because Sacajawea was with them, carrying a baby.

In August of 1805, Sacajawea found
her Shoshoni family. Her brother
was now one of the Shoshoni
leaders. Lewis and Clark traded with
the Shoshoni for supplies.

Sacajawea was sad when she left
the Shoshoni. But she knew that the
explorers needed her help to finish
their journey.

Pacific
Ocean

Fort Mandan

N
W E
S

20

St. Louis

21

22

Finally, on November 7, 1805, the tired group reached the Pacific Ocean. They had never imagined that it could be so beautiful. The hard times were forgotten as they looked at the wonderful sight.

The group stayed in the west for the winter months. They began the return trip when spring arrived. In March 1806, the long trip back east began.

On August 17, 1806, Sacajawea and Toussaint said goodbye to Lewis and Clark. The journey was complete.

Sacajawea, Toussaint, and Pomp went to live in St. Louis, Missouri. They didn't like town life, so they decided to live at Fort Manuel in what is now South Dakota. On December 20, 1812, Sacajawea died from a fever. Today she is remembered as the brave woman who helped Lewis and Clark on their incredible journey.

Glossary

adventure (ad ven'chər) an event that can be exciting

explorer (ek splôr'ər) a person who goes to places that are unknown

incredible (in kred'ə bəl) something that is unusual or special in a way that is hard to believe

kidnap (kid'nap) to take someone away against his or her will

medicine (med'i sin) something used to help a body to heal, take away pain, or treat a disease

supplies (sə plī'z) things needed to do something

About the Author

Irene Nakai Hamilton was born in southern Utah and attended boarding school from the age of six. She attended high school in central Colorado where she enjoyed hiking in the mountains and exploring mountain streams. In 1986, Ms. Hamilton received a degree in Education from Abilene Christian University. She teaches elementary school and lives in a small town in Arizona, in the middle of the Navajo Nation. This book is dedicated to Dawn To'ahani, Dylan K'aayelli, and Tim.

About the Illustrator

Troy Anderson grew up in Oklahoma and Arkansas. A graduate of West Texas State University, Troy has been a professional artist for more than twenty-five years. He has also worked as a teacher, illustrator, painter, and sculptor. His artworks have appeared in many books and magazines. In *Sacajawea,* Mr. Anderson used acrylics to express his unique style.